Terrorism Net Assessment

TERRENCE K. KELLY, DAVID C. GOMPERT, KAREN M. SUDKAMP

Prepared for the Office of the Secretary of Defense
Approved for public release; distribution unlimited

NATIONAL DEFENSE RESEARCH INSTITUTE

For more information on this publication, visit **www.rand.org/t/RRA1929-1**.

About RAND

The RAND Corporation is a research organization that develops solutions to public policy challenges to help make communities throughout the world safer and more secure, healthier and more prosperous. RAND is nonprofit, nonpartisan, and committed to the public interest. To learn more about RAND, visit www.rand.org.

Research Integrity

Our mission to help improve policy and decisionmaking through research and analysis is enabled through our core values of quality and objectivity and our unwavering commitment to the highest level of integrity and ethical behavior. To help ensure our research and analysis are rigorous, objective, and nonpartisan, we subject our research publications to a robust and exacting quality-assurance process; avoid both the appearance and reality of financial and other conflicts of interest through staff training, project screening, and a policy of mandatory disclosure; and pursue transparency in our research engagements through our commitment to the open publication of our research findings and recommendations, disclosure of the source of funding of published research, and policies to ensure intellectual independence. For more information, visit www.rand.org/about/principles.

RAND's publications do not necessarily reflect the opinions of its research clients and sponsors.

Published by the RAND Corporation, Santa Monica, Calif.
© 2023 RAND Corporation
RAND® is a registered trademark.

Library of Congress Cataloging-in-Publication Data is available for this publication.

ISBN: 978-1-9774-1103-7

Cover image: Vertigo3d/Getty Images

About This Report

This report offers a preliminary conception of how to determine the capabilities the United States needs to remain safe from international terrorism. It does so in the light of the U.S. withdrawal from Afghanistan, the decline in threats from major extremist Islamist organizations, and the shift of national security priorities from jihadist terrorism to China and Russia. Notwithstanding these developments, such terrorism could flare anew and differently, suggesting the need to analyze how to assess future threats and what it will take to defeat them. Far from being the final word on this matter, the report is merely an initial think piece to prompt and inform research and more-granular analysis. It does not evaluate the sufficiency of existing U.S. capabilities to combat international terrorism, though it might be of use in any such evaluation. This report should be of interest to national and homeland security professionals.

The research reported here was completed in January 2023 and underwent security review with the sponsor and the Defense Office of Prepublication and Security Review before public release.

RAND National Security Research Division

This research was conducted within the International Security and Defense Policy Program of the RAND National Security Research Division (NSRD), which operates the RAND National Defense Research Institute (NDRI), a federally funded research and development center (FFRDC) sponsored by the Office of the Secretary of Defense, the Joint Staff, the Unified Combatant Commands, the Navy, the Marine Corps, the defense agencies, and the defense intelligence enterprise. This research was made possible by NDRI exploratory research funding that was provided through the FFRDC contract and approved by NDRI's primary sponsor.

For more information on the RAND International Security and Defense Policy Program, see www.rand.org/nsrd/isdp or contact the director (contact information is provided on the webpage).

Acknowledgments

The authors would like to thank Paul Davis and Andy Liepman for their constructive and helpful review of this report. It is better for their efforts. Additionally, Anthony Vassalo provided important insights into how the U.S. government assesses terror threats, which the research team could not have known without his help, and which helped get this report across the finish line.

Summary

The end of U.S. occupations of Afghanistan and Iraq could lessen the incentive of jihadists to attack the United States and its partners in the West. At the same time, the capabilities of al-Qa'ida and the Islamic State of Iraq and Syria (ISIS) to launch attacks are evidently degraded. These developments coincide with sharply heightened U.S. security concerns in the Western Pacific and Eastern Europe, which will and should have first claim on U.S. government policymakers' attention and defense and intelligence resources. However, remnants and offshoots of jihadist-terrorist organizations are still present in the Greater Middle East and Africa; much of the region remains unstable and unpredictable; and anti-Western passions persist in Afghanistan, Syria, the Sahel, and elsewhere. Therefore, future attacks cannot be excluded. If jihadists do attempt to renew international terrorist attacks, they could have better instruments: affordable, lethal unmanned aerial systems (UASs); advanced data networking; artificial intelligence; cyberwar know-how; and biological agents.

Failing to update the tactics and capabilities that worked so well in the years since the terrorist attacks of September 11, 2001, is dangerous. The U.S. government has learned over the past 20 years that threats mutate and mutations can be dangerous if not recognized early. Current conditions might be in a lull. Still, the resources available to combat future jihadist terrorism will presumably be constrained or reprogrammed, given the progress in counterterrorism and competing, higher priorities.

Preparedness in the context of constrained resources demands disciplined analysis. Our preliminary conception for consideration begins with a structured assessment of potential threats and prioritizes counterterrorism capabilities that would reduce the danger of major attack to near zero (taking into account other demands for these capabilities, in other regions, for other purposes).

Thus, as a first step, potential threats can be assessed according to their intent, capabilities, and access to chosen targets. These familiar parameters are especially useful in assessing threats objectively and consistently. Broadly stated, threats might arise along a spectrum from large, geographically concentrated groups to distributed networks of radicalized individuals and cells.[1] Empirically, threats of the former category have the intent and capabilities to conduct very harmful attacks (though consequential attacks from smaller groups are also possible), whereas those of the latter category might have better access, being widely distributed, but less capability and commitment to inflict great harm.

The next step is to enumerate the functions U.S. counterterrorism entities need to perform to prevent attacks. Although we recognize that centralized and decentralized threats will require different functions, these are to gather and analyze intelligence; directly attack terrorists; disrupt terrorists' command, control, and communications; create a hostile environment for international travel of terrorists; deny terrorists safe havens; impede terrorist recruiting; disrupt terrorist financing; enlist and maintain international cooperation; enlist, support, and manage local partners and proxies; fight indefinitely; and protect vital targets. At a time of degraded terrorist groups and constrained resources, the functions involving intelligence and interdiction are likely of highest priority. Other efforts, such as to counter jihadist propaganda and recruiting, deter state sponsorship of terrorist groups, and convince populations not to support them, are also important but outside the scope of this preliminary effort.

Performing high-priority counterterrorism functions requires certain specific means (or instruments). For the purpose of illustration, we provide our assessments of the relative importance of several such means against the assessed threats:

- for intelligence
  - human
  - signals (SIGINT)
  - geospatial
  - general regional (often from open sources)
- for interdiction
  - indigenous combat forces

---

[1] These small groups and individuals can be supported by larger groups, though the challenges posed by individuals who are simply inspired by the ideology of these larger groups and not part of them are different.

- U.S. covert strike assets (special operations forces [SOF] and intelligence community [IC] assets)
- UASs for surveillance and strike
- active cyber tools.

Of these, we believe preliminarily that SIGINT, direct-action SOF, and abundant, affordable, lethal UASs are of particular value.

We do not evaluate whether existing U.S. counterterrorism capabilities are adequate. Although these capabilities and the U.S. personnel who use them have a stellar record, we are in a new and unpredictable era in which the importance of counterterrorism is dwarfed by that of potential conflict with China and Russia. Evaluating current capabilities is a matter for further analysis, taking into account tighter resources going forward, with threats apparently declining or changing and other needs taking precedence. We believe this framework would be of use in analyzing the adequacy of these capabilities.

Our framework offers an indicative assessment of competing demands for high-priority counterterrorism means, especially considering the prioritization of the Indo-Pacific Command area of responsibility in the emerging national defense strategy that seeks to deter war with great powers. Because of their versatile capabilities, covert strike assets (SOF and IC), UASs, and SIGINT are in growing demand elsewhere. The tentative implication of this is that means of particular utility in combating persistent and new terrorist threats could be increasingly scarce in the Greater Middle East, as other regions take on greater importance.

With threats assessed and functions and means to counter them prioritized, it is possible to derive *net* terrorist threat assessments: in essence, the dangers given a determined set of U.S. counterterrorism capabilities. These should align with what the United States would consider minimal acceptable levels of vulnerability: In cases of large high-casualty attacks, that level is zero. In cases of low-casualty, harder-to-prevent attacks from networked small cells and individuals, the acceptable level is rare and minor harm from each attack.

Our preliminary sense that jihadist terrorism could demand capabilities that might be in demand elsewhere argues for further, more-definitive analysis, which should include analyzing the utility of specific capabilities to counter specific threats. Such additional work might also include an evaluation of current and programmed U.S. counterterrorism capabilities to inform acquisition and resourcing priorities going forward.

To be clear, this report does not indicate that a major new terrorism threat looms or that the United States has its geostrategic priorities wrong. Rather, it calls for calm, fresh attention to how to counter terrorist threats, whatever their form and scale, in this new era.

Contents

Figure and Tables

Figure

Tables

CHAPTER 1

Introduction

Motivation

The motivation for this effort is the loss of Afghanistan, the shift in attention and resources of the U.S. national security establishment away from the Central Command (CENTCOM) area of responsibility to that of Indo-Pacific Command (INDOPACOM) and to a lesser extent European Command (EUCOM), and the potential for these shifts to change the dynamics that have enabled the United States to succeed at preventing major terrorist attacks since September 11, 2001 (9/11).

This exploratory report outlines an approach that could complement the already very effective efforts of the U.S. counterterrorism community now that counterterrorism will no longer be the primary focus of U.S. national security planning. We believe that a structured assessment of the adequacy of investments in counterterrorism would help make for clear choices by policymakers and those who make decisions on defense and intelligence community (IC) budgets. In this initial effort, we focus primarily on threats from foreign terrorists (notably, extremist jihadists).

Background and Scope

This report focuses on the threat from jihadist terrorist groups, while recognizing that the challenge is broader than the threat posed by them. The end of the U.S.-led wars in Afghanistan and Iraq could remove the strategic motivation for some jihadist-extremist terrorist organizations to attack the United States. Indeed, there is a consensus in and outside government that terrorist organizations are seriously degraded and the danger of terrorist activity from these groups is much diminished. Still, the persistence of specific conflicts, such as those in Syria, Yemen, and Somalia, could give rise to new attacks. Afghanistan could remain a source of danger. Indeed, the shift in U.S. attention toward China and Russia could be viewed as opportune by terrorist groups that still harbor the goal of attacking the United States and its partners.

Consequently, the U.S. government—in both policymaking and resource allocation—will need to ensure that the resources and capabilities needed to counter terrorism remain adequate and appropriate, even while they are in increasing demand for other missions, such as in the INDOPACOM and EUCOM areas of responsibility in particular. Failure to do so could increase the probability of major attacks, however low it might seem now.

This report outlines a framework for informing decisions concerning what resources to allocate for counterterrorism and on what capabilities. It does not seek to determine definitively what specific counterterrorism instruments should be available. Rather, it illustrates how a risk-based approach that compares U.S. capabilities devoted to the counterterrorism mission and the threat posed by foreign terrorist organizations can yield what we will call a *net* threat assessment. By this we mean levels and types of threats taking into account U.S. efforts designed to defeat or prevent them. This in turn should help those responsible for policy and resourcing decisions understand the relative needs of the different parties seeking policymaker attention and resources.[1]

Such a net assessment of terrorist threats is complicated by the conspicuous asymmetries between terrorists' objectives and capabilities on the one hand and U.S. objectives and capabilities on the other.[2] Not only do terror-

---

[1] Net assessment methodology has a long history in the Department of Defense (DoD) as a method to integrate, analyze, and assess the capabilities and strategies of the U.S. military and a particular adversary. We surveyed the available literature on net assessment; see Paul Bracken, "Net Assessment: A Practical Guide," *Parameters*, Vol. 36, No. 1, Spring 2006; Eliot A. Cohen, *Net Assessment: An American Approach*, Jaffee Center for Strategic Studies, Memorandum No. 29, April 1990; and Institute for Defense Analyses, "Net Assessment: The Concept, Its Development and Its Future," NS P-4748, May 1990. Although the terrorist threat is more challenging to determine than that posed, for example, by a foreign military, the concept is similar.

[2] Brian Michael Jenkins, personal communication with the authors, March 30, 2022. Jenkins (senior adviser to the president at the RAND Corporation) provided us with

ists often have the initiative, but the capabilities needed to conduct terror attacks and those needed to defend against them are exceptionally asymmetric. For example, terrorists only need to attack one undefended target selected from an almost infinite number of targets to be successful, and even in failure they can still succeed by elevating the sense of vulnerability and fear in a population. Opposed to this, the defender needs to be successful everywhere, all the time.

Furthermore, the capabilities needed for some terror attacks are minimal (e.g., a knowledge of where a crowd will gather and access to a motor vehicle, or of an internet connection vulnerable to cyberattack), whereas what is needed to discover and interdict every attack can be enormous and includes not only intelligence and operational capabilities but also the authorities to use them. That said, the most catastrophic attacks require considerable terrorist capabilities, though that could change in the future (e.g., biological attacks). To simplify this problem so that it is tractable and analyzable, we make a few assumptions, articulated in the following chapter.

This report will concentrate on threats from foreign jihadist organizations rather than all threats. This was necessary for our limited effort because it narrows the U.S. capabilities (and authorities) that need to be considered primarily to those of the DoD and IC, as well as to capabilities to identify and interdict threats. Other efforts, such as countering jihadist propaganda and recruiting, deterring state sponsorship of terrorist groups, and convincing populations not to support them, are also important but outside the scope of this preliminary effort. Furthermore, we fully recognize that domestic terrorism is also a threat and that many other counterterrorism actors at the federal, state, and local levels play important roles in the full set of efforts. We believe this approach could have benefits to them as well.

Organization of This Report

Our method to derive net threat assessments can be summarized as follows:

---

a short document capturing key lessons he has developed from more than 50 years studying terrorism. We use these as a key set of inputs shaping our assumptions and framework.

- assess U.S. vulnerability to and potential consequences of terrorist attacks, from concentrated groups to distributed networks
- identify counterterrorism approaches and functions the U.S. government must be able to perform
- identify specific means needed to execute these approaches and conduct these functions (e.g., for intelligence and interdiction), and competing demands for such means, to determine available capabilities
- using this articulation of the threats and U.S. ways and means, provide a net assessment of threats adjusted for available U.S. capabilities to prevent or defeat them.

Accordingly, Chapter 2 presents a way to describe and assess terrorist threats and explains how to derive U.S. vulnerabilities from those threats. This in turn allows us to identify and prioritize key counterterrorism functions to reduce these vulnerabilities to an acceptable level: most importantly, to eliminate the danger of any large-scale, highly consequential attack, such as those that al-Qa'ida committed on and in the period after the terrorist attacks on 9/11. From these crucial functions, we derive and assess specific means, or instruments, notably for intelligence and interdiction. We also offer ways to examine the magnitude, rough costs, and competing demands for these instruments, though details on this will not be covered in this preliminary effort. Chapter 3 presents our preliminary conclusions and recommendations, especially for further research and analysis.

CHAPTER 2

Method

Net Assessment Framework

A net assessment of terrorist threats takes into account the capabilities and intentions of known terrorist organizations and compares them with ways (elements of a strategy) and means (instruments) the United States and its partners might employ to counter them. With an appropriate strategy and suitable and sufficient instruments, a net assessment should match what U.S. policymakers consider to be satisfactory limits on the probability and magnitude of threats, especially the most severe ones.

Figure 2.1 provides an overview of our approach to risks of attack. This risk framework is applicable to both the general terrorism phenomenon and that of countering a specific terrorist organization. We begin with a brief discussion of consequences because those drive many choices that will be important, then discuss how we view threats and vulnerabilities, with the full realization that the goal of the U.S. and partner governments is to defend against all terrorist attacks and that predicting consequences is an inexact business. Nevertheless, events that can be expected to have significant consequences should receive more attention than those of lesser expected consequence, and assessing risk requires some such measure to have value.

Consequences

The consequences of a terrorist attack drive the need for all counterterrorism analysis. Although it is true that before an attack it is difficult to clearly understand what its consequences will be, and the counterterrorism community mostly focuses on preventing terrorist attacks in general,

FIGURE 2.1

Terrorism Net Assessment Framework

Threat ✕	Vulnerability ✕	Consequences

• Threats against
 • U.S. domestically
  • Foreign
   • Jihadi
   • Shia/Iran
  • Domestic
   • Jihadi
   • Non-Jihadi
 • U.S. targets overseas
 • Partners
• Threat intensity (for threat being examined)
• Threat nature
 • Direct strike
 • Recruitment and incitement
	• V = f(U.S. capabilities)
	• V = f(Attention, Resources, Inputs)
	• Attention encompasses political, policy, and operational attention/availability of assets
	• Resources are (at least) budgets and human capital available. Could also require technology over time.
	• Inputs are the products needed for the U.S. capabilities created for the counterterrorism mission to work.
	• Note that these processes differ in important ways for foreign and domestic terrorist threats.
		• Severity of strike
		• Nature of strike (kinetic, bio, etc.)
		• Direct strike or recruiting, or direct and indirect

consequences still drive policy and resourcing decisions. For example, the Transportation Security Administration was created to prevent a 9/11-style attack, and the Department of Homeland Security deploys and operates radiation detectors at some major transportation hubs to prevent nuclear or radiological attacks. These capabilities are in place because these types of attacks would cause significant consequences.

Consequences can be characterized objectively (e.g., casualties, economic damage) and subjectively (e.g., demands from U.S. citizens for their government to protect them that result in investments beyond the need, such as reactions to these calls that have opportunity costs). Objectively speaking, most terrorist attacks are small events; however, they can prove to be major political inflection points and require—in democratic systems of government, at least—efforts that are out of proportion with actual threats and vulnerabilities. Both sets of considerations matter.

For our purposes in this initial effort, we limit ourselves to noting that the U.S. government focuses on minimizing the likelihood of the most consequential attacks. Future analysis should look at a broad set of consequences and use them to estimate and articulate risk.

Threats

We begin with an established and sound threat-assessment framework.[1] The framework considers the intent, capability, and access of terrorist organizations, and it can help policymakers understand the evolution of terrorist groups and how to prioritize the threat from those groups when distributing resources.[2]

The application of this definition across the two ways of viewing the terrorism threat we consider—defined terrorist organizations and terrorism as a mode of political expression—will differ. For the former, there will be discrete capabilities against which U.S. capabilities can be prepared, and a net assessment will look more like the traditional ones used to compare nation-state militaries. For the latter, the comparison will be less quantitative but still essential because it will capture considerations not tied to specific terrorist groups and will be helpful in informing policy, planning, and budget decisions.

Intent

Intent has the following two components: the decision that an attack on a specific target is desired and the operational decision to attempt an attack. The target could be very broad (e.g., an attack on an iconic landmark in the United States without specifying which one), whereas the operational decision is specific, requires certain capabilities, and is subject to the normal decisionmaking processes of organizations about risk and likelihood of success. Intent also applies to combating terrorism as a mode of political expression in that the assessment that there is a threat of attacks of a particular type, even if they are not tied to specific groups, will inform judgments about capabilities needed to thwart them (discussed under Capabilities). It

---

[1] Kim Cragin and Sara A. Daly, *The Dynamic Terrorist Threat: An Assessment of Group Motivations and Capabilities in a Changing World*, RAND Corporation, MR-1782-AF, 2004, pp. 9–11.

[2] Cragin and Daly (2004) restricted intent to "anti-U.S. sentiment" to limit the scope of terrorist organizations that U.S. policymakers should consider.

is useful to keep in mind that intent is not a constant and that a group that poses a threat today might not tomorrow, and vice versa.

The U.S. government's understanding of a terrorist group's intent is a product of intelligence, both classified and open source. The United States, across multiple presidential administrations, has focused attention on those foreign terrorist groups that threaten to attack the U.S. homeland, U.S. interests abroad, or key U.S. partners and allies. Over the past decade, this included Sunni groups such as al-Qa'ida, the Islamic State of Iraq and Syria (ISIS), and certain branches, along with various organizations that receive direct support from Iran (e.g., Lebanese Hizballah, Iraqi Shi'a militia groups, and the Houthi).

Capabilities

Next, we consider the ability of a group to conduct a consequential attack of any specific type on the United States or its domestic or foreign interests. Even if a group expresses the intent to target the United States, if it lacks the personnel, physical and financial resources, infrastructure, and training needed to successful plan for, prepare, and conduct the attack, it lacks the ability to conduct a direct attack against its intended target (though it might still be able to motivate others to do so).

In this framework, there are two categories of capabilities necessary for a terrorist organization: those that sustain the group's existence and those that provide the ability to conduct a specific attack. The first category, *organizational capabilities*, includes such elements as ideology, leadership, recruitment, and publicity.[3] The second, *operational capabilities*, includes such elements as command and control, weapons, operational space, operational security, training, basic intelligence, technical expertise and specialists, external weapon sources, sanctuary, money, and deception skills.[4] There is no simple compilation of organizational and operational capabilities that automatically indicates one group is more of a threat to U.S. interests than another, which is why the intent of a group and its manner of attack must be considered.

---

[3] Cragin and Daly, 2004, p. 26.

[4] Cragin and Daly, 2004, p. 58.

Terrorist capabilities are the objects that the United States can target. Some can be interdicted directly (e.g., money), while others can be countered but not directly interdicted (e.g., ideology). In general, the more organized a terrorist group is and the more it has real operational capabilities, the more touch points exist to attack the organization.

Access to Targets

Access, in this context, implies both physical access and the belief on the part of the terrorist organization that it can succeed with reasonable risk. For example, a terrorist organization that wants to attack a commercial aircraft has to navigate security at the departure airport and factor in the possibility of a federal air marshal who can defeat the attack on the plane. Although air marshals are not on all flights, terrorists must consider the high probability of failure should one be present.[5]

Although terrorist organizations have conducted successful attacks against U.S. interests abroad in the past two decades, a large, coordinated attack against the U.S. homeland has not occurred since 9/11. This is the result of collaboration among U.S. intelligence, law enforcement, and military counterterrorism entities and support from allies and foreign partners. The likelihood that a group will be able to conduct a physical attack causing significant casualties comes down to three things: (1) a target having exploitable vulnerabilities, (2) a terrorist group believing that the risk of attacking a specific target that it believes has exploitable vulnerabilities is acceptable, and (3) the group having the requisite capabilities, which, as we discuss in the next section, are a function of U.S. counterterrorism capabilities.

Reducing Vulnerability to Threats

In an open society, there will always be a wealth of vulnerable targets if viewed in isolation. For example, every large gathering of people has some level of vulnerability. However, because U.S. counterterrorism efforts have

---

[5] Morral and Jackson use this example (Andrew R. Morral and Brian A. Jackson, *Understanding the Role of Deterrence in Counterterrorism Security*, RAND Corporation, OP-281-RC, 2009).

been so successful, we view *vulnerability*, or the probability of a successful attack, at its most basic sense as function of U.S. capabilities: how they are deployed and how they are perceived by terrorists (Figure 2.1). The absence of consequential foreign attacks within the United States since 9/11 indicates that, as long as U.S. capabilities are maintained, appropriately deployed, and perceived as such by terrorists, they have a high chance of deterring or preventing major attacks.

We use the "ends, ways, means" terminology that is standard in U.S. military planning for discussing strategies, and because vulnerability is a direct function of U.S. capabilities, we begin with a strategy for developing those capabilities. In this technical language, *ways* are typically an articulation of a strategy for what needs to be done. In the following section, we propose 11 ways.

Counterterrorism Functions

RAND research provides insights into what functions the United States needs to be able to perform to reduce vulnerability. These functions address not only attacks from known terrorist groups but also the potential for terrorist attacks from unanticipated groups, or, as discussed earlier in the section on Threats, terrorism as a mode of political expression.[6] The first ten are useful for limiting the effectiveness of terrorists, and the 11th for protecting prospective targets:

1. gather detailed intelligence, which facilitates all other capabilities and is the most important
2. disrupt a group's ability to command and control its elements and to communicate
3. disrupt a group's ability to finance itself and, in particular, to raise and move money
4. subject international movement of people, materials, and money to interdiction

---

[6] This list was provided by Brian Michael Jenkins as a summary of his insights from more than 50 years of terrorism studies (March 30, 2022). Some items are articulated differently here than in his input, but the core concepts come from this communication. The 11 items are listed in the Appendix.

5. eliminate safe havens
6. impede recruitment
7. take direct actions against terrorists so they cannot operate safely
8. enlist, support, and manage indigenous proxies
9. enlist and maintain international cooperation and partners as a key facilitator to all of the actions above
10. continue the struggle indefinitely
11. protect vital targets and make them more resilient.[7]

Specific Means of Counterterrorism

The next step is to consider the means, or instruments, needed to perform such critical functions. For now, we focus primarily on intelligence and DoD-led interdiction instruments. The discussion that follows is meant to illustrate the approach, not make definitive statements about which means are most important.

To illustrate how this works, we assume that the terrorist threat will persist and that these threats could well extend to the United States and its partners.[8] Table 2.1 illustrates types of counterterrorism instruments in relation

---

[7] We adapted this list from Brian Jenkins' subject-matter expertise and additional RAND research. See also Seth G. Jones and Martin C. Libicki, *How Terrorist Groups End: Lessons for Countering al Qa'ida*, RAND Corporation, MG-741-1-RC, 2008, pp. 123–139; and Ben Connable and Martin C. Libicki, *How Insurgencies End*, RAND Corporation, MG-965-MCIA, 2010, pp. 151–156. These categories are broad, and each could—and in another document perhaps should—be expounded on. For example, item nine in this list certainly contains efforts to convince partners and allies to adopt policies and practices that mitigate the root causes of terrorist activity if possible. Indeed, Brian Jenkins, who provided this list, has written about such efforts (Paul K. Davis and Brian Michael Jenkins, *Deterrence and Influence in Counterterrorism: A Component in the War on al Qaeda*, RAND Corporation, MR-1619-DARPA, 2002). See also Paul K. Davis, Eric V. Larson, Zachary Haldeman, Mustafa Oguz, and Yashodhara Rana, *Understanding and Influencing Public Support for Insurgency and Terrorism*, RAND Corporation, MG-1122-OSD, 2012, for a robust discussion of such items.

[8] There is little reason to expect that the overall jihadist threat to the United States, its interests, and friends will increase; indeed, it could decrease. With U.S. and allied occupations of Muslim countries virtually ended (except for a small number of trainers in Iraq), the motivation of protecting Islam from "the West" has dissipated to some degree.

to two types of threats—centralized and decentralized—using our experience and insights rather than research into current practice. We articulate major categories of instruments within these two major categories (intelligence and interdiction) because of their frequent use in previous counterterrorism efforts. We postulate their importance against two major types of terrorist threats. The importance of a type of capability to counter a type of threat is indicated by High, Medium, and Low.

Although Table 2.1 is a simplification meant to illustrate an approach, assessing and prioritizing the means to combat certain specific threats would be more complex and use more-nuanced methods.

Importance is not the only factor that should be considered; it is also necessary to factor in cost. Costs for these various instruments are not calculable at the level of analysis possible in this effort, though we can assert that especially heavy requirements could cause high actual and opportunity costs. Even the loosest approximations of cost raise the question of what to include.

TABLE 2.1

Illustrative Importance of Major Types of U.S. Counterterrorism Instruments Against Types of Threats

U.S. Instruments	Centralized Threats[a]	Decentralized Threats[b]
Indigenous forces	High	Low
U.S. covert strike (SOF and IC)	High	Low
UASs with precision strike	High	Low
Internet/cyber presence and influence	Medium	High
HUMINT and general regional intelligence	High	Low
GEOINT	High	Low
SIGINT	High	High

NOTE: GEOINT = geospatial intelligence; HUMINT = human intelligence; SIGINT = signals intelligence; SOF = special operations forces; UAS = unmanned aerial system.
[a] Territorial safe havens for sizable groups within a small number of ungoverned or hostile countries.
[b] Radicalized small cells and individuals throughout the international system, dependent on social media.

Because of the recent shift in focus to conflicts with China and/or Russia rather than the terrorist threat, it is likely that the largest concern with availability of intelligence and interdiction assets is that demands elsewhere (e.g., INDOPACOM and EUCOM) would limit available assets, and this could present significant opportunity costs. A particular concern is that GEOINT and SIGINT could be pulled toward other missions, leaving counterterrorism without adequate means. Table 2.2 illustrates our assessment of possible competition for assets that have proven important in the counterterrorism fight, using our experience and insights.

What this discussion illustrates is that there will be increased demand for the means required to perform the counterterrorism functions that U.S. intelligence and military forces have performed so well since 9/11. The key question, then, is whether there will be sufficient means to execute the counterterrorism strategies of the nation. Although there are competent agencies and talented people working on this problem, we believe an assessment of this sort, with detailed analysis to support it, would help illustrate critical needs for policymaking and resource allocation.

Net Assessment

A net assessment takes into account U.S. abilities to counter specific threats and to do the things necessary to counter terrorism as a means of political expression. Although this last category sounds nebulous, it is also necessary. For example, the United States and its North Atlantic Treaty Organization (NATO) allies created significant economic and military challenges for Russia in Ukraine through indirect means; might Russia support terrorist organizations who aspire to attacks on the United States to (1) exact revenge and (2) cause the United States to expend resources countering the threat? Maintaining the focus and ability to identify and negate emerging threats is critical, especially those that could produce significant consequences.

Net assessments, then, have at least two manifestations: the comparison of means needed to counter known threats and the means required for vigilance. The sum of these, understanding that many capabilities can be used against more than one threat at a time, would indicate the U.S. instruments needed to keep the country safe.

TABLE 2.2

Required Counterterrorism Means Versus Demands of Other Combatant Commands

Asset	Counterterrorism	INDOPACOM and EUCOM
Aircraft carriers and wings	Low	High
Land-based tactical air	Low	High
Land-based strategic air	Low	High
Naval combatants and submarines	Low	High
Strategic deterrent forces	Low	High
Covert strike assets (SOF and IC)	High	High
UASs (ISR and strike)	High	High
Space-based C4ISR, including GEOINT	Low	High
HUMINT and general regional intelligence	Medium	High
SIGINT	High	High
Internet monitoring and proactivity (information operations)	High	Medium
Cyber operations	Medium	High

NOTE: C4ISR = command, control, communications, computers, intelligence, surveillance, and reconnaissance; ISR = intelligence, surveillance, and reconnaissance.

Importantly, net assessments are not just about a quantitative comparison of capabilities. An important factor in examining terrorist capabilities is whether terrorists perceive them to be sufficient to overcome U.S. counterterrorism ways and means. This is more than just a straight alignment of terrorist and U.S. capabilities and how they stack up. Judgments on both sides are critical. In this regard, deterrence is a critical factor in affecting the decisionmaking process of a terrorist organization (especially whether and how to mount an attack) and thus should be part of U.S. planning.[9] We do

[9] Andrew Morral and Brian Jackson (2009) provide an important framework for understanding deterrence in this context.

not examine deterrence in this effort, but if terrorists perceive U.S. counter-terrorism preparations as strong enough to make an attack extremely risky, then their intent is positively affected, the threat declines, and risk is lower. However, it is the perception of exceptional preparedness, created by investments in attention, resources, and enablers, that lowers risk, and decreasing these investments might be harmful. Subsequent research should examine this component of terrorism net assessments.

The next logical step in this process is to conduct net assessments for known serious terrorist threats and to articulate those assets needed to counter the more general threats discussed previously. Because this is an exploratory effort with limited resources, we provide only an outline of what is needed rather than an actual application of the method to real threats, as follows:

- For each known threat determined to be sufficiently grave by U.S. counterintelligence agencies, the Office of the Director of National Intelligence and National Counter Terrorism Center should coordinate U.S. government efforts to
  - identify types of attacks that have consequences that must be prevented (e.g., another 9/11-type attack, biological terror, nuclear terror). Any successful terror attack is deplorable, but not all represent strategic failures.
  - identify terrorist organizations that pose the greatest threats, and for each
    - characterize the threat as discussed above
    - characterize their intent, capabilities, and access to targets
    - identify elements of their organization or operations that can be attacked with available U.S. capabilities (means) and prioritize these to achieve the maximum effect
    - identify aspects of the targets they threaten (vulnerabilities) that could be hardened or otherwise made more difficult or resilient to attack.
- For each of the 11 ways discussed above
  - identify the means needed to make them successful against known and potential terrorist organizations (as discussed)

- identify the means needed to prepare for those more-general threats. This will take the form of capabilities needed in different areas of the world and globally that collectively pose a general threat, as discussed, but do not individually rise to the level of an identified terrorist organization that the United States wants to take on. It also includes the professional estimates of those unknown threats.

- For all of these articulated requirements for U.S. capabilities, assess how they overlap and how capabilities could serve multiple threats (e.g., strike assets in a particular theater of operations are likely sufficient to address many threats there).

- This collection of requirements would then be compared to assets likely to be available to the counterterrorism efforts of the various elements of the U.S. government (and its partners) to indicate whether the means available are sufficient and to highlight areas in which risk might be unacceptable.

CHAPTER 3

Conclusions and Further Work

As promised at its outset, this report provides an outline of how to perform net assessments of current and future international terrorist threats, taking into account counterterrorism functions the U.S. government must perform and means it must possess. The criterion for judging what functions and instruments are required is to all but eliminate the probability of a major attack and to make less significant attacks difficult for terrorists to carry out.

To perform such a net assessment, the intent, capabilities, and access to targets of chosen terrorist threats must be analyzed. For our preliminary purposes, we suggest concentrating such analyses on two broad classes of threats: very capable, usually large, anti-American jihadist extremist groups (mainly in and around the Greater Middle East) and widely, if not globally, distributed networks of radicalized small cells or individuals.[1] Of the two classes, the first is currently the more capable of carrying out highly destructive attacks. Terrorist groups, whether centralized or decentralized, might have access to advanced means to facilitate attacks: increasingly affordable and available UASs; data networking, artificial intelligence, and cyber know-how; and, possibly, biological agents.

To keep the danger of very destructive attacks at or near zero, the United States must be able to perform certain essential functions and possess certain related and especially effective means to defeat terrorists and prevent attacks. These, like other counterterrorism means, are likely to be in demand

---

[1] These small groups and individuals can be supported by larger groups, though the challenges posed by individuals who are simply inspired by the ideology of these larger groups and not part of them are different. Small groups could be capable of very consequential attacks.

for other, higher priority national security preparations, especially those involving China and/or Russia, which would indicate the need for trade-offs in planning, programming, budgeting, and deployments. Because key counterterrorism capabilities highlighted here are unlikely to be big-ticket items and are both very versatile and fungible, our preliminary take is that today's prioritizations of potential threats in East Asia and Europe do not preclude using these capabilities to prevent major terrorist attacks (such as those that could originate in the Greater Middle East), though competition for resources makes them less available.

Our purpose in preparing this preliminary report is to prompt and inform further, definitive work. A complete net assessment should include examination of other threats by intent, capabilities, and access, and the potential for distributed threats to become more dangerous (e.g., offensive cyber threats or bioterrorism). It could also define minimal levels of support and include recommendations on mechanisms to ensure that resources—and the counterterrorism capabilities they enable—do not fall below an analytically defensible threshold. Follow-on work is needed to perform the quantitative and qualitative analysis to validate or fill in data and assessments called for by this preliminary work. Defining specific risks from the full array of terrorist organizations of interest and the capabilities needed to defend against unknown threats (e.g., what agencies are responsible for what; what policies, programs, budgets and forces they need; and how these can best be arrayed against the threat) would provide the input needed to create defensible net assessments.

A full research effort to develop and test a net assessment approach like that proposed here would require working closely with the U.S. defense and intelligence counterterrorism community to implement the steps outlined at the end of Chapter 2. Some of those steps are straightforward (for example, identifying and analyzing the capabilities and organizational characteristics of those terrorist groups that pose especially grave threats). Some of the steps might require the development of formal analytic methods and models, such as modeling and simulation to determine the ability of intelligence and strike assets owners to fill taskings in different parts of the globe, and models for what means are adequate for meeting threats of various types. These analytic methods are not unique, though there could be unique applications that would need to be developed. Furthermore, this approach should be expanded to address not just foreign terrorist threats emanating from the Greater Middle East but also the full portfolio of likely terrorism threats.

With U.S. counterterrorism resources likely to be further constrained in the future, it is timely to revisit the functions Western and regional allies can perform, the capabilities within their reach, and the ways the United States can increase coalition counterterrorism activities.

Eleven Capabilities

Brian Michael Jenkins shared a summary of his observations regarding the critical capabilities the United States and partners need to maintain to reduce and manage the risk from terrorist threats using more than 50 years of research on the topic. The following are the 11 capabilities as they appeared in Jenkins' communication, dated March 30, 2022.

Ability to Obtain Detailed Intelligence

In my view, this is perhaps the most important capability, and it is prerequisite to the success of many of the others. To deal with groups operating internationally, multilateral collaboration, beyond traditional allies, is required. One of the major achievements of the effort against al-Qa'ida was the unprecedented cooperation among intelligence services and law enforcement organizations worldwide. Maintaining that capability requires continuing nurturing. "Intelligence" here is used in its broadest sense to also include detailed knowledge of the society or subculture from which the terrorist group has emerged, and the beliefs, mindset, and operational code of the terrorist group itself.

Ability to Directly Attack Terrorists

Nowhere can be safe. To be able to arrest, capture, or kill terrorist leaders, cadre, and operatives requires specially trained and equipped forces and the use of precision military technology (cruise missiles, UASs, airstrikes, special operations). Success here depends on having detailed intelligence.

Ability to Disrupt Terrorists' Command, Control, and Communications

This can be achieved by removing terrorist leaders, keeping them on the run, making it dangerous for them to communicate. It will not stop self-selecting individuals from carrying out terrorist attacks in support of a cause or ideology, but it can degrade the ability of a targeted group to mount more-ambitious operations.

Ability to Create a Hostile Environment for International Movement of Terrorists

This was essential in dealing with al-Qa'ida immediately after 9/11. It means increasing the risks of moving people, moving money, or communicating.

Ability to Deny Terrorists Safe Havens

This was the initial objective of the GWOT [Global War on Terrorism], America's post-9/11 diplomacy with Pakistan, and later, Operation Inherent Resolve. It can be achieved by deterring state sponsors and assisting weaker allies, although it may not be feasible to eliminate all ungoverned spaces.

Ability to Impede Terrorist Recruiting

What we are talking about here is the ability to prevent the creation of a large organization. Large numbers are not needed for operational purposes, but large numbers provide a reservoir of talent that enables the terrorists to conduct more-ambitious operations. Impeding terrorist recruiting also involves political warfare or psychological operations by creating counter-terrorist narratives. The internet has provided terrorists with the ability to manage a global terrorist enterprise, attract volunteers, and remotely recruit terrorist operatives—it has become a new theater of conflict, and must be calculated as part of a net assessment.

Ability to Disrupt Terrorist Financing

Individual terrorist operations require little money; larger sums are needed to sustain a large organization and operate at a more sophisticated level. Counterterrorist abilities here include financial intelligence to identify and discourage sources of funding and their ability to transfer funds.

Ability to Enlist and Maintain International Cooperation

Successfully countering an international terrorist threat requires creating supportive alliances, which, in turn, requires demonstrated adherence to values. It may also involve offering military assistance.

Ability to Enlist, Support, and Manage Local Partners and Proxies

Committing U.S. ground forces significantly raises the costs and risks U.S. casualties, which quickly exhaust U.S. patience. Locally recruited allies have frequently proved effective. Recent examples include the enlistment of Afghan tribes in toppling the Taliban in 2001, the enlistment of Sunni tribes in Anbar Province in Iraq, and the use of the primarily Kurdish Syrian Democratic Forces to conduct the ground campaign against Islamic State. Efforts in this dimension may also include out-recruiting terrorist organizations and inducements to turn members of terrorist organizations.

Ability to Fight Indefinitely

Time is a precious commodity. Counterterrorist campaigns are long slogs. The Red Army Faction in Germany and Red Brigades terrorist campaigns lasted the better part of two decades. The IRA [Irish Republican Army] terrorist campaign in the United Kingdom went on for 25 years. It has been more than 30 years since the creation of al-Qa'ida and 27 years since it declared war on the United States. Superior military resources (or increased ruthlessness) do not readily reduce the time horizons. Public support for counterterrorist efforts tends to be episodic—a major terrorist attack like 9/11 creates public pressure for a military response, but memories soon fade, and initially popular campaigns become "forever wars." A net assessment must include the ability to enlist and maintain public support (or reduce costly deployments).

Ability to Protect Vital Targets Against Attack

Physical security measures are necessary and have effect, but they are costly and disruptive, and they can have adverse effects on society. Vulnerabilities are infinite, resources are not. The U.S. government must confine security enhancements to those that provide a "net security benefit," that is, they do not simply displace the risk. The U.S. government cannot destroy a terrorist group on the basis of security alone.

Abbreviations

9/11   September 11, 2001
DoD   Department of Defense
EUCOM   European Command
GEOINT   geospatial intelligence
HUMINT   human intelligence
IC   intelligence community
INDOPACOM   Indo-Pacific Command
SIGINT   signals intelligence
SOF   special operations forces
UAS   unmanned aerial system

Bibliography

Bergen, Peter, David Sterman, and Melissa Salyk-Virk, "Terrorism in America 18 Years After 9/11," *New America*, September 18, 2019.

"Berlin Christmas Market Attack," DW, December 17, 2021. As of April 21, 2022:
https://www.dw.com/en/berlin-christmas-market-attack/av-60158240

Bracken, Paul, "Net Assessment: A Practical Guide," *Parameters*, Vol. 36, No. 1, Spring 2006.

Callimachi, Rukmini, Katrin Bennhold, and Laure Fourquet, "How the Paris Attackers Honed Their Assault Through Trial and Error," *New York Times*, November 30, 2015.

Cohen, Eliot A., *Net Assessment: An American Approach*, Jaffee Center for Strategic Studies, Memorandum No. 29, April 1990.

Connable, Ben, and Martin C. Libicki, *How Insurgencies End*, RAND Corporation, MG-965-MCIA, 2010. As of February 10, 2023:
https://www.rand.org/pubs/monographs/MG965.html

Cragin, Kim, and Sara A. Daly, *The Dynamic Terrorist Threat: An Assessment of Group Motivations and Capabilities in a Changing World*, RAND Corporation, MR-1782-AF, 2004. As of February 10, 2023:
https://www.rand.org/pubs/monograph_reports/MR1782.html

Davis, Paul K., and Brian Michael Jenkins, *Deterrence and Influence in Counterterrorism: A Component in the War on al Qaeda*, RAND Corporation, MR-1619-DARPA, 2002. As of February 10, 2023:
https://www.rand.org/pubs/monograph_reports/MR1619.html

Davis, Paul K., Eric V. Larson, Zachary Haldeman, Mustafa Oguz, and Yashodhara Rana, *Understanding and Influencing Public Support for Insurgency and Terrorism*, RAND Corporation, MG-1122-OSD, 2012. As of February 10, 2023:
https://www.rand.org/pubs/monographs/MG1122.html

Doxsee, Catrina, Jared Thompson, and Grace Hwang, "Examining Extremism: Islamic State Khorasan Province (ISKP)," Center for Strategic and International Studies, September 8, 2021. As of March 21, 2022:
https://www.csis.org/blogs/examining-extremism/
examining-extremism-islamic-state-khorasan-province-iskp

Goillandeau, Martin, and Kara Fox, "Man Arrested in Connection with 2017 Manchester Arena Bombing," CNN, October 22, 2021. As of April 21, 2022:
https://www.cnn.com/2021/10/22/uk/manchester-arena-bombing-man-arrested-gbr-uk-intl/index.html

Institute for Defense Analyses, "Net Assessment: The Concept, Its Development and Its Future," NS P-4748, May 1990.

INTERPOL, "Notices," webpage, undated. As of April 18, 2022:
https://www.interpol.int/en/How-we-work/Notices

Jadoon, Amira, Abdul Sayed, and Andrew Mines, "The Islamic State Threat in Taliban Afghanistan: Tracing the Resurgence of Islamic State Khorasan," *CTC Sentinel*, Vol. 15, No. 1, January 2022.

Jones, Seth G., and Martin C. Libicki, *How Terrorist Groups End: Lessons for Countering al Qa'ida*, RAND Corporation, MG-741-1-RC, 2008. As of February 10, 2023:
https://www.rand.org/pubs/monographs/MG741-1.html

Kapur, Roshni, "The Persistent ISKP Threat to Afghanistan: On China's Doorstep," Middle East Institute, January 6, 2022.

Mir, Asfandyar, "The ISIS-K Resurgence," Wilson Center, October 8, 2021. As of March 21, 2022:
https://www.wilsoncenter.org/article/isis-k-resurgence

Morral, Andrew R., and Brian A. Jackson, *Understanding the Role of Deterrence in Counterterrorism Security*, RAND Corporation, OP-281-RC, 2009. As of February 10, 2023:
https://www.rand.org/pubs/occasional_papers/OP281.html

"Nice Attack: What We Know About the Bastille Day Killings," *BBC News*, August 16, 2016. As of April 21, 2022:
https://www.bbc.com/news/world-europe-36801671

Office of the Director of National Intelligence, *Annual Threat Assessment of the U.S. Intelligence Community*, February 7, 2022. As of April 18, 2022:
https://www.dni.gov/files/ODNI/documents/assessments/ATA-2022-Unclassified-Report.pdf

Seldin, Jeff, "Islamic State, Al-Qaida Building Support in Afghanistan, Report Says," *VOA News*, February 15, 2022. As of March 21, 2022:
https://www.voanews.com/a/islamic-state-al-qaida-building-support-in-afghanistan-report-says-/6443700.html

Sherwood-Randall, Liz, "Remarks as Prepared for Delivery by Assistant to the President for Homeland Security, Dr. Liz Sherwood-Randall on the Future of the U.S. Counterterrorism Mission: Aligning Strategy, Policy, and Resources," speech delivered at the Atlantic Council, Washington, D.C., September 8, 2021. As of April 18, 2022:
https://www.whitehouse.gov/briefing-room/speeches-remarks/2021/09/09/remarks-by-assistant-to-the-president-for-homeland-security-dr-liz-sherwood-randall-on-the-future-of-the-u-s-counterterrorism-mission-aligning-strategy-policy-and-resources/

Soliev, Nodirbek, "The April 2020 Islamic State Terror Plot Against U.S. and NATO Military Bases in Germany: The Tajik Connection," *CTC Sentinel*, Vol. 14, No. 1, January 2021. As of March 21, 2022: https://ctc.westpoint.edu/the-april-2020-islamic-state-terror-plot-against-u-s-and-nato-military-bases-in-germany-the-tajik-connection/

U.S. Department of the Treasury, "Treasury Designates Key Financial Facilitator for the Islamic State's Afghanistan Branch," press release, November 22, 2021. As of April 18, 2022: https://home.treasury.gov/news/press-releases/jy0502

U.S. Senate, *Senate Armed Services Committee Hearing on the Posture of United States Central Command and United States Africa Command, March 15, 2022*, Washington, D.C., March 15, 2022. As of April 18, 2022: https://www.centcom.mil/MEDIA/Transcripts/Article/2968166/senate-armed-services-committee-hearing-on-the-posture-of-united-states-central/

Yardley, Jim, Katrin Bennhold, Michael S. Schmidt, and Adam Nossiter, "Mounting Clues Point to Brothers and Trip to Syria," *New York Times*, November 16, 2015.

Zengerle, Patricia, and Jonathan Landay, "CIA Chief Highlights Loss of Intelligence Once U.S. Troops Leave Afghanistan," Reuters, April 14, 2021. As of April 18, 2022: https://www.reuters.com/world/asia-pacific/cia-chief-says-intelligence-will-diminish-once-us-troops-leave-afghanistan-2021-04-14/